DISCOVERING THE CARIBBEAN
History, Politics, and Culture

BAHAMAS

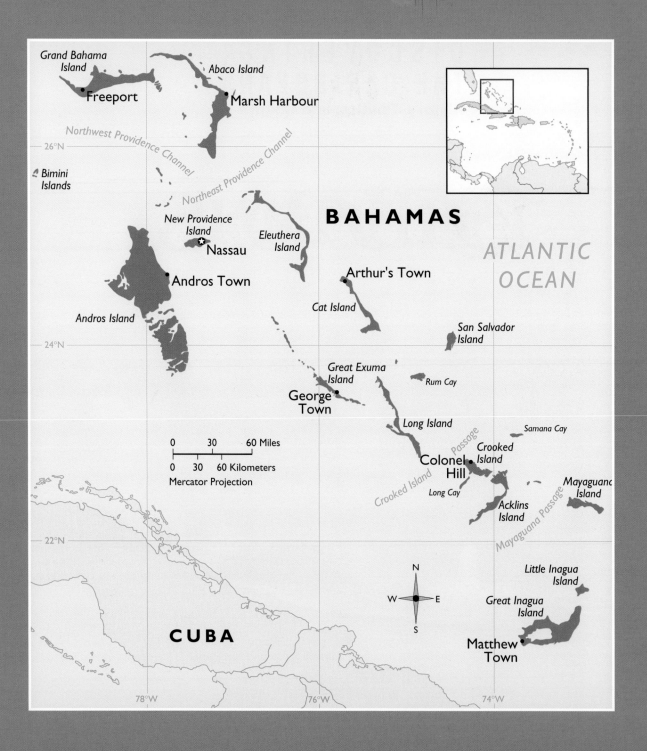

DISCOVERING THE CARIBBEAN
History, Politics, and Culture

BAHAMAS

Colleen Madonna Flood Williams

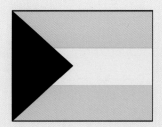

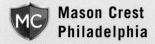

Mason Crest
Philadelphia

Mason Crest
450 Parkway Drive, Suite D
Broomall, PA 19008
www.masoncrest.com

Printed and bound in the United States of America.

CPSIA Compliance Information: Batch #DC2015.
For further information, contact Mason Crest at 1-866-MCP-Book.

First printing
1 3 5 7 9 8 6 4 2

Library of Congress Cataloging-in-Publication Data
        on file at the Library of Congress

        ISBN: 978-1-4222-3316-0 (hc)
        ISBN: 978-1-4222-8633-3 (ebook)

Discovering the Caribbean: History, Politics, and Culture series ISBN: 978-1-4222-3307-8

DISCOVERING THE CARIBBEAN: History, Politics, and Culture

Bahamas	Cuba	Leeward Islands
Barbados	Dominican Republic	Puerto Rico
Caribbean Islands:	Haiti	Trinidad & Tobago
Facts & Figures	Jamaica	Windward Islands

TABLE OF CONTENTS

KEY ICONS TO LOOK FOR:

 Words to Understand: These words with their easy-to-understand definitions will increase the reader's understanding of the text, while building vocabulary skills.

 Sidebars: This boxed material within the main text allows readers to build knowledge, gain insights, explore possibilities, and broaden their perspectives by weaving together additional information to provide realistic and holistic perspectives.

 Research Projects: Readers are pointed toward areas of further inquiry connected to each chapter. Suggestions are provided for projects that encourage deeper research and analysis.

 Text-Dependent Questions: These questions send the reader back to the text for more careful attention to the evidence presented there.

 Series Glossary of Key Terms: This back-of-the book glossary contains terminology used throughout this series. Words found here increase the reader's ability to read and comprehend higher-level books and articles in this field.

DISCOVERING THE CARIBBEAN

James D. Henderson

THE CARIBBEAN REGION is a lovely, ethnically diverse part of tropical America. It is at once a sea, rivaling the Mediterranean in size; and it is islands, dozens of them, stretching along the sea's northern and eastern edges. Waters of the Caribbean Sea bathe the eastern shores of Central America's seven nations, as well as those of the South American countries Colombia, Venezuela, and Guyana. The Caribbean islands rise, like a string of pearls, from its warm azure waters. Their sandy beaches, swaying palm trees, and balmy weather give them the aspect of tropical paradises, intoxicating places where time seems to stop.

But it is the people of the Caribbean region who make it a unique place. In their ethnic diversity they reflect their homeland's character as a crossroads of the world for more than five centuries. Africa's imprint is most visible in peoples of the Caribbean, but so too is that of Europe. South and East Asian strains enrich the Caribbean ethnic mosaic as well. Some islanders reveal traces of the region's first inhabitants, the Carib and Taino Indians, who flourished there when Columbus appeared among them in 1492.

Though its sparkling waters and inviting beaches beckon tourists from around the globe, the Caribbean islands provide a significant portion of the world's sugar, bananas, coffee, cacao, and natural fibers. They are strategically important also, for they guard the Panama Canal's eastern approaches.

The Caribbean possesses a cultural diversity rivaling the ethnic kaleido-scope that is its human population. Though its dominant culture is Latin American, defined by languages and customs bequeathed it by Spain and France, significant parts of the Caribbean bear the cultural imprint of

A windsurfer rides the waves off Harbour Island.

Northwestern Europe: Denmark, the Netherlands, and most significantly, Britain.

So welcome to the Caribbean! These lavishly illustrated books survey the human and physical geography of the Caribbean, along with its economic and historical development. Geared to the needs of students and teachers, each of the eleven volumes in the series contains a glossary of terms, a chronology, and ideas for class reports. And each volume contains a recipe section featuring tasty, easy-to-prepare dishes popular in the countries dealt with. Each volume is indexed, and contains a bibliography featuring web sources for further information.

Whether old or young, readers of the eleven-volume series DISCOVERING THE CARIBBEAN will come away with a new appreciation of this tropical sea, its jewel-like islands, and its fascinating and friendly people!

(Opposite) Tourists stroll the beach on Paradise Island. (Right) Palm trees and turquoise waters off the coast of Nassau, the capital city of the Bahamas. Although together Nassau and Paradise Island (which are connected by bridge) make up less than 2 percent of the total land area of the Bahamas, 60 percent of Bahamians live there.

1 ISLANDS AND CAYS

THE NATION OF the Bahamas is made up of 700 islands and *cays* lying to the southeast of Florida. Bordered on the north and east by the Atlantic Ocean and on the south and west by the Gulf Stream, the Bahamas are not technically part of the Caribbean.

New Providence and Grand Bahama are perhaps the best known of the islands that make up the Bahamas. The largest of the islands is Andros, a major bonefishing destination. Both Harbour Island and Eleuthera are famous for their fantastic pink sand beaches. Other large islands include Cat Island, Long Island, Crooked Island, and Mayaguana Island.

Several island groups are also part of the Bahamas. Closest to Florida's coast are the Bimini Islands. The Exuma Islands consist of more than 365 cays and islands totaling 130 square miles (337 square kilometers). The Abaco

Islands are popular with boaters. Lesser-known islands, known as the "out islands," attract fewer visitors.

The coral islands of the Bahamas are all relatively flat. Some have slight rolling hills, but most do not rise much above sea level. The highest point in the Bahamas, on Cat Island, is Mount Alvernia. It is only 206 feet (62.8 meters) above sea level.

CLIMATE OF THE ISLANDS

The Bahamas enjoys a tropical maritime climate moderated by the warm waters of the Gulf Stream. From December to April (winter in the Bahamas), the average temperature throughout the islands is 70°F (21°C). Evenings are slightly cooler. The temperature on an average Bahamian summer day is 80°F (27°C).

The rainy season in the Bahamas lasts from May to November. The Bahamas experience an average rainfall of 52 inches (132 centimeters) per year. The islands to the north receive a larger amount of this rainfall than do the islands in the south. February and March are the nation's driest months.

Words to Understand in This Chapter

cay—a small, low-lying island or small reef of sand or coral.
fauna—animal life.
flora—plant life.

Hurricane season in the Bahamas officially runs from June to November, but most hurricanes occur between the months of August and September. On average, five hurricanes churn through the Bahamas per year. However, this number can vary greatly from year to year.

PLANTS AND ANIMALS

The *flora* of the Bahamas is unique, vibrant, and diverse. There are over 1,370 species of trees and plants on the islands. Native Bahamian plants include the bull vine, the wild grape, several kinds of fig, and bromeliads. Trees include wild tamarind, pigeon plum, and casuarina pine.

Dolphins leap from the water off Grand Bahama Island as a man pilots a skiff nearby.

The government of the Bahamas has set aside land for 12 nationally funded nature parks. These parks protect and preserve such animals as the Abaco parrot, West Indian flamingos, and green turtles, as well as such natural wonders as undersea caves and coral reefs.

The fauna of the Bahamas is limited. It includes 12 species of native bats, all of them endangered. The only other land mammal native to the islands is the endangered hutia, a member of the rodent family similar to the guinea

pig. Raccoons live in the wild but are not native to the Bahamas. They were brought to the islands during the 1920s by American rum smugglers, who kept them as pets. Escaped raccoons prospered.

Marine mammals can be seen in the waters surrounding the islands of the Bahamas. Humpback whales pass by the Bahamas as they migrate to their mating grounds. Blue whales are commonly sighted off the shores of the islands as well. Tourists and residents alike enjoy watching the antics of Atlantic bottlenose dolphins and revel in rare sightings of the Atlantic spotted dolphin.

The Bahamas are home to 44 species of reptiles and 10 species of snakes. Lizards are abundant throughout the islands. Geckos climb almost everywhere quite easily, while blue-tailed lizards quickly dash to and fro.

The waters around the Bahamas are home to a great variety of sea life, such as this Nassau Grouper.

Quick Facts: The Geography of the Bahamas

Location: chain of islands in the North Atlantic Ocean, southeast of Florida
Area: (slightly smaller than Connecticut)
total: 5,382 sq miles (13,940 sq km)
land: 3,880 sq miles (10,070 sq km)
water: 1,494 sq miles (3,870 sq km)
Borders: none
Climate: tropical marine; moderated by warm waters of Gulf Stream
Terrain: long, flat coral formations with some low rounded hills

Elevation extremes:
lowest point: Atlantic Ocean—0 feet
highest point: Mount Alvernia, on Cat Island—206 feet (63 meters)
Natural hazards: hurricanes and other tropical storms that cause extensive flood and wind damage

Source: CIA World Factbook 2015.

Vegetarian iguanas munch leafy plants, fruits, and berries on the less inhabited outlying islands and cays.

At least 230 species of birds can be seen at various times of the year in the Bahamas. Many of them travel from North America to winter in the tropical maritime climate. Others, like the Bahamas parrot and the woodstar hummingbird, are resident year-round.

TEXT-DEPENDENT QUESTIONS

1. How many islands make up the nation of the Bahamas?
2. What is the name of the largest island in the Bahamas?
3. How many unique species of trees and plants can be found in the Bahamas?

(Opposite) Christopher Columbus and his crew claim San Salvador for Spain, October 12, 1492. Columbus believed the Bahamas were part of an archipelago that lay north of Japan. (Right) Perry Christie, prime minister of the Bahamas, speaks at a United Nations summit on climate change in September 2014.

2 PIRATE'S PARADISE

RECENT ARCHAEOLOGICAL EVIDENCE suggests that the Bahamas may have been settled as early as the fourth century CE. But little is known about these earliest native inhabitants.

In the 9th or 10th century, a group of Arawak Indians known as the Lucayans arrived. The word *Lucayans* comes from the native term *lukku-caire*, which means "island people." These peaceful people may have traveled to the Bahamas in order to avoid conflicts with the Caribs, a *cannibalistic* tribe that was growing more and more dominant in South America as well as in many areas of the Caribbean.

The Lucayans lived in villages that were organized into *clans*. Each clan had a chief (*cacique*). The Lucayans ate fish and shellfish. They planted and harvested vegetables such as corn and yams, and they used a starchy plant known as manioc to make bread.

Life was relatively easy in the islands, so the Lucayans had time enough to develop various skills and crafts. They became expert weavers, making hammocks and clothing to trade with the residents of neighboring islands. They were also accomplished boat builders and carvers. They learned to make pottery, ropes, and even rugs.

Words to Understand in This Chapter

amnesty—a pardon given by a government or government official, usually to a large group of people.

cannibalistic—having the inclination to eat the flesh of other human beings.

clan—a group of people descended from a common ancestor.

founder—to become disabled or sink.

galleons—large Spanish ships used for trade or warfare during colonial times.

Loyalist—one who is loyal to a particular cause, especially an American who favored the British crown during the Revolutionary War era.

ne'er-do-wells—idle or worthless people.

Orient—the Far East, including China and Japan.

privateer—a ship armed and licensed by a government to attack and plunder enemy ships; or a captain or sailor on such a ship.

salvager—one who recovers valuable commodities from wreckages and ruins.

subsistence farmers—farmers who grow enough only to feed their families, with no surplus crops that can be sold.

wrecker—in the history of the Bahamas and the Caribbean, one who lured ships toward the shore in order to wreck them and plunder their cargo.

ARRIVAL OF THE SPANISH

In early August of 1492, three ships under the command of Christopher Columbus departed from Spain on a journey that, Columbus hoped, would take them to the *Orient*. The lands of the East had goods that Europeans coveted, such as spices and silks. But reaching these faraway trade centers required a dangerous overland journey across Asia or a long sea voyage south around the western coast of Africa and then northeast across the Indian Ocean. Columbus hoped to find an easier, more direct route by sailing west across the Atlantic Ocean.

On the morning of October 12, 1492, more than a month after they had last set foot on dry land, Columbus and several of his top officers waded ashore on a small island that they assumed to be near Japan. In reality, the island was in the Bahamas. Columbus named the island San Salvador, claimed it for Spain, and declared the island's native inhabitants to be subjects of the Spanish king and queen. It was about 500 years since the Lucayans had first settled in the Bahamas.

After deciding that the Bahamas contained little of value, the Spaniards removed many of the native Lucayans to work in the gold mines of Hispaniola, a large Caribbean island Columbus had found during his 1492 expedition. (Hispaniola is the site of the present-day nations of Haiti and the Dominican Republic.) Within 25 years, the peaceful Lucayans had virtually disappeared, having fallen victim to European diseases to which they had no immunity, overwork, mass executions, and general mistreatment at the hands of the Spanish.

Soon the Spanish completely abandoned the Bahamas. Greater riches, such as gold and silver, were to be found in Central and South America. Many Spanish *galleons* carrying treasure back to Spain passed through the Bahamas, however, and quite a few *foundered* in violent storms or were wrecked on the reefs of the treacherous waters. In addition, pirates and adventurers plied the area and preyed on the Spanish treasure ships.

ENGLAND CLAIMS THE BAHAMAS

In 1629, King Charles I of England claimed the Bahamas and granted them to an English nobleman, Sir Robert Heath. Nevertheless, the islands remained sparsely populated.

In the late 1640s, about 100 English Puritans under the leadership of a man named William Sayles arrived in the Bahamas. The Puritans were a Protestant religious group who objected to, and were often persecuted by, the official Church of England. Sayles and his followers, who had come from Bermuda, initially landed on the present-day Abaco Island. But the group moved on to Cigatoo Island, whose name they changed to Eleuthera, from the Greek word for freedom. Later they established a settlement on New Providence Island. After weathering some initial difficulties, including the loss of all their provisions and political disagreements, the Puritan settlers established their own independent republic.

For the king of England, the fate of a tiny Puritan republic in the Bahamas was of little concern. Wishing to shore up support for the crown in the aftermath of the English Civil War, King Charles II in 1670 granted the Bahamas to six noblemen, called lords proprietors, who had earlier been granted the Carolinas, in the present-day American states of North and South Carolina. Charles also helped to send to the Bahamas 300 settlers who pledged loyalty to the monarchy.

A Lawless Place

In 1666, four years before Charles's grant of the Bahamas, a settlement named for him had been founded on the island of New Providence. Charles Town soon became a magnet for pirates and outlaws. This was due in part to its fine harbor, and in part to the absence of real authority in Charles Town. The noblemen who had received the Bahamas grant did not actually live there, and the governors they sent to administer their lands were weak and ineffective. The city of Charles Town became a rowdy, lawless place, a home for thieves, prostitutes, and pirates.

In 1684, the Spanish—with whom the British were frequently at war throughout the 17th and 18th centuries—destroyed Charles Town. But the people of the city quickly rebuilt their settlement.

For a certain type of person, the Bahamas could provide a good livelihood. Charles Town was home to many *salvagers*. These men combed the shores for wrecked treasure ships and picked through their remains. Some went a bit further in their quest for easy riches. Called *wreckers*, they lured ships laden with gold and other treasures onto the rocky reefs by placing lights there. When the unsuspecting captain of a ship passing at night saw one of the lights, he would assume it was a distant lighthouse and that his vessel was at a safe distance from the land. After a ship ran aground, the wreckers would board the vessel and confiscate its cargo by force.

In 1695, Charles Town changed its name to Nassau to honor the current King of England, William III. King William III had formerly been the prince of Orange-Nassau.

During this period, England's navy was stretched thin by constant battles with the French and Spanish. As a result, England began to hire *privateers*—private ship captains licensed by the government to attack enemy ships and settlements in the Caribbean. When they plundered a Spanish town or preyed on a French ship, the British privateers kept the treasures they collected—making them little different from pirates.

In 1701, when the Spanish War of Succession broke out, Spain and France allied against England. Together the two nations destroyed Nassau in 1703. Once again, however, the resilient community of pirates, privateers, and *ne'er-do-wells* rose up and rebuilt their city.

Now, however, the outlaw population of Nassau demanded officially what they had to a certain extent enjoyed unofficially: independence. They declared Nassau a "Privateer's Republic," and for a time the rowdy city remained a true pirate's paradise, with no functioning government authority.

In 1717, however, the king of England officially assumed civil and military authority over the islands (though it would be 70 years before the lords proprietors surrendered their rights on the Bahamas to the crown). In 1718, the king appointed a former privateer to the position of royal governor of the islands. Woodes Rogers took his post seriously. Governor Rogers coined a motto in Latin that summed up his mission (and that would eventually embellish the official seal of the Bahamas): *Expulsis Piratis—Restituta Commercia* ("Pirates Expelled—Commerce Restored").

A statue of Woodes Rogers (1679–1723), the first British royal governor of the Bahamas, stands in front of the British Colonial Hotel, Nassau. Once Rogers arrived in the Bahamas in 1718, he succeeded in virtually eliminating pirates from the region.

Woodes guaranteed that all pirates who surrendered would receive *amnesty*. He also promised that those who did not surrender would be treated harshly: their ships would be sunk, and they, if captured, would be executed. Hundreds of pirates did surrender. Most of the rest perished in battle with the governor's naval forces, were hanged, or fled the Bahamas. The era of the Bahamas pirates had come to a bloody end, and Britain was now firmly in control of the colony.

AMERICA AND THE BAHAMAS

Later in the 18th century, Britain would have more trouble with its overseas colonies—but this time no easy solution would present itself. In April 1775, skirmishes in the Massachusetts colony ignited the American Revolution.

The following year, with the war for independence raging on the American mainland, a force of American patriots seized Nassau.

In 1782, a year after the Revolutionary War had ended with the British surrender at Yorktown, Virginia, the Bahamas were surrendered to Spain. But Britain regained control of the islands through a treaty concluded in 1783, and the Bahamas immediately received a new wave of immigrants: Americans who remained loyal to the British crown. Many of these *Loyalists* who had left the newly independent United States came from North and South Carolina. And many intended to re-create in the Bahamas the cotton plantations they had known in America. As in the American South, a plantation economy in the Bahamas would require abundant slave labor. Many slaveholders from the Carolinas brought their slaves with them to the islands, and in the last 25 years of the 18th century, the islands were a major stopping point in the trans-Atlantic slave trade. African slaves—as well as free blacks, many of whom were themselves slaveholders—soon made up a large proportion of the Bahamas' population.

On August 1, 1834, slavery was abolished throughout the British Caribbean colonies. In the Bahamas, many former slaves became fishermen or *subsistence farmers*. A minority of white colonists retained control of the political and economic fate of the islands.

A significant part of the economic activity in the Bahamas once again came to revolve around less-than-reputable work. By 1850, Nassau was once again home to a community of wreckers. The English colonial government set up strict laws to govern "salvaging," but most of these laws had to do with the splitting of the bounty. The government took an immediate 15 percent share of all sales of salvaged commodities, and the governor himself collected 10 percent. With government backing, many wreckers grew bold enough to begin luring ships onto the rocks once more. Still others struck bargains with disloyal seamen who helped to arrange shipwrecks for the purpose of plundering cargo.

From 1861 to 1865, during the American Civil War, residents of the Bahamas found another source of income: blockade running. In order to squeeze the Confederacy (the rebellious Southern states) economically, the Union, with its superior navy, imposed a naval blockade. Foreigners attempting to trade with the South risked having their cargoes confiscated or their ships sunk. In addition to hitting the Confederacy hard, the blockade hurt Great Britain, whose textile industry depended on cotton grown in the

Tourists from the United States buy coconuts and fruit from a vendor in Nassau, circa 1900.

American South. Daring Bahamians saw an opportunity to get rich. They outfitted fast boats to make the dangerous 560-mile (901 km) journey between Nassau and Charleston, South Carolina. They would bring British-made goods into Charleston and carry cotton—which they could trade with the British in Nassau—out. The blockade runners who evaded the Union navy made enormous sums of money, and the Bahamas prospered. But with the end of the Civil War in 1865, the lucrative business disappeared, and hard times befell the islands.

Fortunately for Bahamians, another smuggling opportunity arose in 1919. In that year, the Eighteenth Amendment to the U.S. Constitution—which prohibited the manufacture, transport, and sale of alcoholic beverages—was passed. Demand for alcohol in the United States remained high, however, and those who wanted to take some risks could make huge profits. Nassau became a center for rumrunners, as the liquor smugglers were called, and once again the Bahamas enjoyed a measure of prosperity. When the Twenty-first Amendment was passed and Prohibition ended in 1933, however, the Bahamas suffered a major economic blow. That blow was made worse several years later by the loss of another important source of income for Bahamians: diving for sponges. In 1938, disease ravaged local sponge beds, and more islanders were cast into poverty.

ECONOMIC PROGRESS

World War II (1939–45) pumped money into the Bahamian economy. The United States signed a lease for a naval base on Mayaguana Island in 1940, and the British maintained an air base on New Providence.

THE BAHAMAS' MOST FAMOUS GOVERNOR

In 1940, a new British governor arrived in the Bahamas. He was Edward VIII, and in 1936 he had served as England's king. But Edward's decision to marry a divorced American woman named Wallis Simpson—a choice unacceptable to the British government—had forced him to give up his throne. As the duke of Windsor, he was the governor of the Bahamas until 1945.

After the war, tourists—particularly from the United States and Canada—began to visit the Bahamas in large numbers. American tourism to Cuba ceased shortly after the Communist regime of Fidel Castro came to power there in 1959—and many vacationers who previously went to Cuba discovered the Bahamas. The newly established Bahamas Development Board led a massive effort to lure tourists to the islands, and it paid off: by 1968, one million tourists had visited the Bahamas.

INDEPENDENCE

During the late 1960s, a movement for independence from Great Britain gained momentum in the Bahamas. One of its leaders was a black Bahamian politician named Lynden Pindling, who in 1953 had helped found the Progressive Liberal Party (PLP) to oppose the white colonialist United Bahamian Party. In 1967, Pindling became the premier of the Bahamas colony, and over the next six years he steered his homeland toward independence. On July 10, 1973, the islands of the Bahamas officially became the Commonwealth of the Bahamas, an independent country within the British

Commonwealth of Nations.

Pindling served as prime minister of the Bahamas until 1992. During his long career in public service, he was credited with helping to improve educational and economic opportunities for Bahamians. But he was also dogged by allegations of bribery and charges that his government turned a blind eye toward—and perhaps was even bankrolled by—Colombian drug lords. Drug trafficking, drug use, and crime in general began to increase in the Bahamas in the 1980s.

In 1992, with his popularity undermined by the assorted allegations, Pindling and his Progressive Liberal Party were defeated at the polls by the conservative Free National Movement (FNM). FNM leader Hubert A. Ingraham became prime minister; Ingraham was elected to another five-year term in 1997.

Damaged houses on Eleuthera Island the day after Hurricane Floyd pounded the Bahamas in September 1999. Abaco Island was also hit hard by the storm.

In 1999, the islands were hit by two particularly devastating hurricanes, Dennis and Floyd. Together, these two hurricanes destroyed homes and wreaked havoc on the economy of the Bahamas. In 2005 another powerful storm, Hurricane Wilma, resulted in significant flooding on Grand Bahama Island and caused damage on several smaller islands. In 2012, Hurricane Sandy killed two people and caused $700 million in damage in the Bahamas.

Hubert Ingraham served as prime minister of the Bahamas from August 1992 to May 2002, and held the position again from May 2007 to May 2012.

In elections held in May 2002, the PLP came to power once again, and Perry Christie replaced Ingraham as prime minister. The FNM defeated the PLP in May 2007, and Ingraham returned as prime minister for a third term. In elections held in 2012, the PLP regained power and Christie was returned to the post of prime minister. As a result of the election defeat, Ingraham resigned as leader of the FNM, and Hubert Minnis was chosen to lead the party.

TEXT-DEPENDENT QUESTIONS

1. What British royal governor drove pirates out of the Bahamas in the 18th century?
2. What event helped to increase tourism in the Bahamas during the 1960s?
3. What black Bahamian politician helped steer the country to independence in 1973?

(Opposite) A cruise ship prepares to enter Nassau harbor. Tourism is a major part of the Bahamas' economy, and employs approximately half of the country's workforce. (Right) A fish market at the docks of Potter's Cay near downtown Nassau.

3 A Tourism-Driven Economy

THE ECONOMY OF THE Bahamas is driven primarily by tourism, but it is supplemented by banking, agriculture, fishing, and manufacturing. The illegal smuggling of cocaine, from Colombia into the United States via the Bahamas, also pumps millions of dollars into the Bahamian economy.

The Bahamian economy is small when compared to other countries. In 2014 the country's *gross domestic product (GDP)*—the total value of goods and services produced annually in the country—was about $11.4 billion, which is less than many American states. But Bahamians enjoy a relatively high standard of living, especially when compared with many of their Caribbean neighbors. For example, the average working-class Bahamian earns five times more than a college-educated teacher in Jamaica. In the

Bahamas, GDP per capita, a rough equivalent of average annual income per citizen, is estimated at $32,000 in 2014. Worldwide, this falls within the high-income range.

TOURISM AND SERVICES

The lifeblood of the Bahamian economy is tourism, which along with tourism-driven construction and manufacturing accounts for approximately 60 percent of the country's gross domestic product. Tourism and related activities employ roughly 50 percent of the archipelago's labor force.

In 2014, an estimated 5.7 million tourists visited the islands. Cruise ship companies consistently list the Bahamas as the number-one tourist destination for the Caribbean.

The Bahamas is also an important center for international finance and insurance activity. More than 400 banks from over 35 nations do business within the Bahamas. The islands are known as an international *tax haven*, because the tax rate is very low. Because the Bahamas will not allow financial

 Words to Understand in This Chapter

gross domestic product (GDP)—the total value of goods and services produced in a country annually.
subpoena—to serve or summon with a writ to appear in court.
tax haven—a place that provides opportunities for individuals or businesses to shelter their money from taxation.

records to be *subpoenaed* by other governments, many businesses and individuals have used the commonwealth as a convenient location for hiding money and assets from their own governments. In 2014, banking and finance generated about 15 percent of the annual GDP.

Agriculture and Manufacturing

Only about 5 percent of Bahamians are involved in farming. Small quantities of pineapples are grown on the islands. Citrus fruits and some vegetables are grown in Great Abaco for export to the United States, United Kingdom, Switzerland, and Denmark. Pigeon peas, tomatoes, cucumbers, onions, and potatoes are grown commercially in North Andros and sold to those same four export partners.

A produce vendor poses at her stand in the farmer's market at Freeport on Grand Bahama Island.

Quick Facts: The Economy of the Bahamas

Gross domestic product (GDP*): $11.4 billion (2013 est.)

GDP per capita: $32,000 (2013 est.)

Inflation: 1%

Natural resources: salt, aragonite, timber, arable land

Agriculture (2% of GDP): citrus fruits, vegetables, poultry

Services (91% of GDP): tourism, banking, government

Industry (7% of GDP): tourism, banking, oil bunkering, maritime industries, transshipment, salt, rum, aragonite, pharmaceuticals

Foreign trade (2014):
Exports: $960 million: crawfish, aragonite, crude salt, polystyrene products
Imports: $3.245 billion: machinery and transport equipment, manufactures, chemicals, mineral fuels; food and live animals

Currency exchange rate: $1 Bahamian = U.S. $1 (fixed rate)

*GDP = the total value of goods and services produced in one year.
Figures are 2014 estimates unless otherwise indicated. Sources: CIA World Factbook 2015.

Conchs are caught for local consumption. Fresh fish are a locally consumed food product as well. The major export of the fishing industry is lobster.

Beer and rum are manufactured on New Providence and exported to other countries. Salt and petrochemicals are also manufactured in the Bahamas for the export market. The pharmaceutical industry contributes a growing share to the country's gross domestic product.

CHANGES FOR WORKERS

Unemployment has been a chronic problem in the Bahamas. In the late 1990s, as the global economy was strong, unemployment decreased dramatically,

Tourist resorts like the Atlantis Hotel on Paradise Island create many jobs.

falling ffrom 14.8 percent in 1992 to about 7 percent by 2002. However, in 2008-09, a worldwide economic recession began affecting the unemployment rate in the Bahamas, and it increased from 7.6 percent in 2008 to over 14 percent by 2010. By 2014, the unemployment rate had reached a record 15.4 percent. The government has attempted to implement policies to improve this, but thus far they have not taken hold.

TEXT-DEPENDENT QUESTIONS

1. What is the lifeblood of the economy of the Bahamas?
2. Why have international banking and finance become an important sector of the Bahamian economy?

(Opposite) Port Lucaya Marketplace is a colorful collection of shops and restaurants on Grand Bahama Island. (Right) A group of Bahamian children gather on a porch.

4 Urban Islanders and Family Islanders

THE POPULATION OF the Bahamas is made up of a mix of races, including blacks, whites, Asians, and Hispanics. In addition to differences in race and ethnicity, Bahamians are divided socially and economically by their status as either "urban islanders" or "family islanders."

About 90 percent of Bahamians are black. Most are descended from slaves brought from North and South Carolina after the American Revolution. The ancestors of these slaves were primarily members of the Ibo, Mandingo, or Yoruba tribes and lived originally in West Africa. Not all blacks who immigrated to the Bahamas came as slaves, however. Some came as freemen. These black freemen often owned their own black slaves. Others were runaway slaves, intent on finding independence and freedom.

In recent years, many blacks from Haiti, one of the world's poorest countries, have entered the Bahamas illegally in search of jobs. Bahamians have relegated them to poor-paying manual labor. Haitians are widely resented by the general public; they are looked down upon for many reasons, including their darker skin and shorter stature.

White Bahamians, who make up almost 5 percent of the population, are primarily of English and Irish descent. Small numbers of Bahamians claim Greek descent; most are related to divers who arrived in the islands to hunt for sponges, and then remained. Other groups of white Bahamians are direct descendants of the pirates and wreckers who inhabited Nassau during its "Privateer's Republic" days.

Asians and Hispanics together make up about 3 percent of the population. They are for the most part well integrated into Bahamian society.

URBAN ISLANDERS

The residents of Nassau and Freeport, the islands' two largest cities, are primarily professional, upper-middle-class, and working-class Bahamians.

Words to Understand in This Chapter

libel—published statements or representations that convey an unjustly unfavorable impression of a person.

obeah—a West Indian religion with roots in Africa, characterized by the use of magical rituals and herbal medicines.

Here, islanders are employed in the tourism, banking, and service industries. Young people wear the same sort of clothing that you might see American teenagers wearing.

Recreation for these urban Bahamians is varied. Many love to play and watch games of basketball or soccer. Others enjoy boating and water sports. Some like to barbecue. Still others like dancing. Almost all urban islanders love beauty pageants, and many contests—for both men and women—are held throughout the year.

FAMILY ISLANDERS

The outlying, or "Family Islands," are home to quite a different breed of Bahamian. The residents of the Family Islands are, economically speaking, members of the Bahamas' lower class. Most are fishers or subsistence farmers and are much less "modern" than their city cousins. Many are skilled at weaving straw baskets. The *obeah* religion, which is characterized by a belief in sorcery and magic ritual, is widely practiced.

The lives of so-called family islanders aren't so hard that they can't find time for recreation, however. They tell folktales that have been passed down through generations. They lounge in the sun and wade

An Anglican priest performs a service in a hundred-year-old church in Albert Town, Long Cay. Albert Town today is uninhabited. Most people of the Bahamas are Christian, and about one-fifth of Bahamians follow the Anglican faith.

in the ocean. They especially love to celebrate family events such as births and weddings with grand, lively parties.

RELIGION

The Anglican Church, or Church of England, is the official church of the Bahamas. Other Christian denominations include Baptists, Catholics, and Methodists.

Men and women dress up for church each Sunday. Singing voices echo across the islands, often to the accompaniment of electric guitars, basses, and keyboards, drums, and tambourines. Most Bahamians view church service as more than a weekly religious obligations; for them it is a social event not to be missed.

A bowl of pig feet souse, a popular native dish, served in a restaurant on Grand Bahama Island.

EDUCATION IN THE BAHAMAS

School attendance is required for Bahamian children between the ages of 5 and 16. Most primary and secondary education in the Bahamas is provided by public schools, though there are some private and parochial schools as well. Primary and secondary schools are well attended. All students in the Bahamas wear school uniforms, and each school district has its own uniform colors. Public preschools were introduced

Quick Facts: The People of the Bahamas

Population: 321,834

Ethnic groups: black 90.6%, white 4.7%, black and white 2.1%, other 1.9%, unspecified 0.7% (2010 est.)

Age structure:
0–14 years: 23.2%
15–64 years: 69.8%
65 years and over: 7%

Population growth rate: 0.87%

Birth rate: 15.65 births/1,000 population

Death rate: 7 deaths/1,000 population

Infant mortality rate: 12.5 deaths/1,000 live births

Life expectancy at birth: 71.93 years
male: 69.48 years
female: 74.46 years

Total fertility rate: 1.97 children born per woman

Religions: Protestant 69.9% (includes Baptist 34.9%, Anglican 13.7%, Pentecostal 8.9% Seventh Day Adventist 4.4%, Methodist 3.6%, Church of God 1.9%, Brethren 1.6%), Roman Catholic 12%, other Christian 13% (includes Jehovah's Witness 1.1%), other 0.6%, none 1.9%, unspecified 2.6% (2010 est.)

Languages: English, Creole (among Haitian immigrants)

Literacy rate (age 15 and older who can read and write): 95.6% (2003 est.)

Source: CIA World Factbook 2015.

throughout the nation beginning in the late 1990s.

There are four schools for higher education in the Bahamas. The government- run College of the Bahamas, which has campuses in Nassau and Freeport, offers courses of study in banking, finance, sciences, arts, and humanities. The University of the West Indies has a regional branch located in Nassau; it is respected throughout the Caribbean for its fine Centre for Hotel and Tourism Management. Also located in the city are the Bahamas Technical and Vocational Institute and the Bahamas Hotel Training College, which teaches students the skills necessary to work in the hotel and service industries.

A drummer performs on Paradise Island.

THE MEDIA

The Broadcasting Company of the Bahamas (BCB) is a government-owned but commercially run broadcasting company. The BCB operates four major radio stations and Bahamas Television, which services Nassau, New Providence, and the Central Bahamas.

Bahamians have access to four daily newspapers (the *Bahamas Journal*, the *Freeport News*, the *Nassau Guardian*, and the *Tribune*) and one semiweekly newspaper (the *Punch*). Reporters have enjoyed freedom to print the news, despite the commonwealth's strict **libel** laws.

MUSIC

Goombay is the most uniquely Bahamian style of music. It is played using a piano or a guitar that is accompanied by a wide variety of percussion instruments—usually handmade goatskin rattles, drums, and maracas, as well as cowbells. The wind instruments of *Goombay* music are often made from conch shells, though standard flutes and pipes are also common. The word *Goombay* comes from an African word that means "beat" or "rhythm," and drums form a vital part of the music.

Since the days of slavery, *goombay* has been played in the Bahamas by so-called rake and scrape bands. The original rake and scrape bands used improvised instruments because slaves could not afford traditional ones. Drums were typically made from goatskin stretched over the top of a pork barrel. To create a distinctive scraping sound, a metal file was run across a carpenter's saw. A washtub with a string through it that was tied to a long stick functioned as a kind of violin. Today's rake and scrape bands supplement their sound with modern instruments like the electric guitar and the saxophone, but the feel of the old music remains.

One other type of Bahamian music deserves mention: religious music. Some hymns that can be heard today at a Bahamian religious service resemble American slave spirituals—not surprising, since many slaves were brought to the Bahamas from the American South in the late 18th century. Gospel, another musical form associated especially with African –Americans, is popular in Bahamian religious services. But then, so too are traditional European hymns—a reflection of the diverse influences that have shaped the Bahamian people and their culture.

 ## TEXT-DEPENDENT QUESTIONS

1. What percentage of Bahamians over age 15 can read and write?
2. What style of music is unique to the Bahamas?

(Opposite) The harbor at Hope Town, on Elbow Cay. (Right) A small town on Man o' War Cay. Both are part of the Abaco Islands group in the Bahamas.

5 CITIES AND DISTRICTS

THERE ARE TWO major cities in the Bahamas: Nassau and Freeport. Nassau, the nation's capital, is located on New Providence Island. Home to about 250,000 residents, it is the largest city in the Bahamas.

Nassau was once infamous for its resident pirates and privateers. Today, though it is a world-recognized financial center, Nassau is also known as a center for *money laundering*—the moving of cash through a series of transactions designed to conceal the fact that it was made through illegal activities such as drug trafficking.

Freeport, the second-largest city in the Bahamas, is located on Grand Bahama Island. Among the city's attractions is the Garden of Groves, which features 5,000 plants and shrubs. Rand Memorial Nature Center is a great place for visitors and residents of Freeport to get away from it all and take a quiet nature hike.

The Commonwealth of the Bahamas is divided into 21 political districts. Below are overviews of a few of the districts.

ACKLINS AND CROOKED ISLAND DISTRICT

This political district is made up of Crooked Island, Acklins Island, Long Cay, Samana Cay, and Plana Cays. The Bight of Acklins is known for its tarpon, a large, bony fish prized by sport fishermen. The Plana Cays are a series of cays whose nature reserves are home to endangered hutias and iguanas.

BIMINI DISTRICT

The Bimini islands, which are home to around 2,000 people, were made famous by the American writer Ernest Hemingway, who summered there during the 1930s. His novel *Islands in the Stream* is a ***semi-autobiographical*** account of the time he spent in the Biminis.

Words to Understand in This Chapter

semi-autobiographical—a written work that blends elements from the author's life with fictional elements.
money laundering—processing stolen or dishonest money in order to conceal where it originally came from.

An aerial view of Spanish Wells, a fishing town on Eleuthera Island.

Today the Bimini District is a favorite haunt of Florida college students on spring break. It is also one of the few places in the world where the rare Atlantic spotted dolphin can be seen in the wild. On occasion, lucky visitors even get to swim with these playful sea mammals.

CAT ISLAND

This island district has a population of about 1,500. Once known as San Salvador, the island got its present name, locals say, from the infamous pirate Arthur Catt. Some residents of Cat Island still practice slash-and-burn agriculture. Many also still practice bush medicine and the African religion of obeah. Cat Island includes the highest point in the Bahamas, Mount Alvernia (also known as Como Hill), which rises to 206 feet (63 m).

EXUMAS

With a population of about 7,500, the district of Exumas is composed of two main islands: Great Exuma and Little Exuma. In addition, there are a total of 365 cays in this district. Some of these cays have come under government protection and are now known collectively as the Exuma Cays Land and Sea Park.

FREEPORT

The Freeport district includes Grand Bahama Island. Next to New Providence island, it is the most visited island in the Bahamas. Forty acres (16 hectares) of this island have been set aside for the Lucayan National Park. The park encompasses natural treasures from both the land and the sea, including mangrove trees and a large underwater cave system.

LONG ISLAND

The southern cape of Long Island is an excellent area to snorkel and enjoy coral reefs. The town of Stella Maris on Long Island is best known for its great scuba diving and fishing opportunities. The lagoons near McKann's Bay are an excellent destination for bird-watchers. Bat lovers can visit Cartwright's Caves.

A small boat makes its way past fine homes on one of the Bimini islands.

MARSH HARBOUR

Named for the largest town in the Abaco Islands, this district is the second-largest landmass in the Commonwealth of the Bahamas. The main island in this district is Abaco Island. Because it is covered with a forest composed of pine trees and shrubs, Abaco Island attracts many birds. The waters surrounding Abaco and the Abaco Cays boast impressive coral reefs. Walkers Cay sits along the edge of the Gulf Stream and is famous for its awesome

This is one of two bridges that connect Paradise Island with the city of Nassau on New Providence Island.

sports fishing. Bird-watchers, divers, and fishermen all enjoy this island and its district.

NEW PROVIDENCE

This district is home to the nation's capital city, Nassau. Here visitors can enjoy all the modern conveniences of the United States and other large developed nations—while still soaking up the easygoing charm of the Bahamas. Attractions include the Straw Market, where islanders sell handmade straw goods and woodcarvings, and Historic Bay Street, which features shops, pubs, and restaurants along its wide brick sidewalks.

New Providence's architecture is a mix of Old World and New World elements. A statue of Queen Victoria, England's legendary 19th-century monarch, stands watch over Parliament Square. This particularly historic part of the city's downtown area includes the nation's legislative and Supreme Court buildings, as well as the Nassau Public Library and Museum. Fort Fincastle, completed in 1793 by the British royal governor Lord Dunmore, sits atop a hill east of the government buildings; the fort is shaped like a ship. By contrast, Cable Beach—located a few miles west of Nassau— is home to modern luxury resorts, shops, a golf course, and a large casino.

North of Nassau, and connected to the capital by two bridges, is Paradise Island. A favorite vacation spot of the very wealthy, it is known especially for its posh resorts, glitzy casinos, and scenic golf courses. Of course, Paradise Island also has something that has been drawing tourists to all the Bahamas for more than half a century—miles of beautiful, sun-kissed beaches and crystal-clear water

TEXT-DEPENDENT QUESTIONS

1. On what island is the capital city, Nassau, located?
2. What is the second-largest city in the Bahamas?
3. How many cays are included in the Exumas district?

January

Junkanoo, a festival that begins just before dawn on New Year's Day, is a celebration of African culture.

March

Commonwealth Day is celebrated the second Monday in March.

April

Easter (which in some years falls in March) is the most important religious occasion for Bahamian Christians.

May

Whitmonday, the day after the Christian religious feast of Pentecost, is a traditional holiday throughout British lands. It falls seven weeks after Easter.

June

The first Friday in June is **Labour Day**, which honors working men and women.

July

July 10, **Independence Day**, commemorates the day in 1973 when the Bahamas gained independence from Great Britain.

August

The first Monday in August is **Emancipation Day**. It marks the freeing of all African slaves in the Bahamas, which took place in 1834.

October

October 12, **Discovery Day**, is a celebration of Christopher Columbus's arrival in San Salvador in 1492.

December

Like Christians everywhere, Bahamians celebrate **Christmas** on December 25.

Boxing Day, a traditional English holiday, is celebrated on the 26th.

Members of the Bahamas Junkanoo Revue on parade. Junkanoo is a style of music named after a Bahamian slave who used his music and colorful clothing to cheer other slaves.

Conch Salad

2 large conchs
1/2 tsp hot pepper
2 tomatoes
1 cucumber
1/2 cup sour orange juice
1 bell pepper
1 onion
2 tsp lime juice
Salt and pepper to taste

Directions:

1. Wash conchs with a mixture of lemon, salt, and water.
2. Clean and cut conchs into small cubes
3. Toss in mixing bowl with remaining ingredients and serve.

Cassavas

3 fresh cassavas
4 cloves minced garlic
1/2 tsp salt
1/2 cup olive oil
Lemon juice

Directions:

1. Add cassavas and salt to pot of water and boil for 30 minutes or until tender.
2. Remove cassavas from pot.
3. Sprinkle with garlic and lemon juice.
4. Pour heated olive oil over cassavas and serve.

Grouper Chowder

2 lbs boneless grouper
1 medium onion, chopped
2 ribs celery, chopped
1 medium bell pepper, minced
2 medium chopped potatoes
4 cups diced tomatoes
5 cups fish stock
1/2 tsp thyme
1/2 tsp allspice
2 Scotch Bonnet chilies
1 bay leaf
1 tbsp lime juice
Salt and pepper to taste
1 tbsp seasoning salt

Directions:

1. Dice the fish into half-inch pieces and place in mixing bowl.
2. Marinate with lime and spices and refrigerate for 2–3 hours.
3. Bring fish stock to a boil.
4. Add all ingredients and simmer for 1 hour, stirring occasionally.

Grilled Fish

Olive oil
2 large garlic cloves
1 1/2 tbsp fresh lime juice
1 tbsp ginger
1 chili, seeded and thinly sliced
Four 6-oz. fish fillets
Salt and pepper

Directions:

1. Combine olive oil with garlic, lime juice, ginger, and chili.
2. Place fish fillets in the mixture. Coat fillets well with mixture. Cover and refrigerate for 1 hour.
3. Remove the fillets from the marinade. Remove the excess garlic and ginger.
4. Season the fish with salt and pepper and cook over grill.

Johnny Cakes

1 cup flour
1/2 cup cornmeal
1 egg, beaten
5 tsp baking powder
1/3 cup sugar
2 tbsp vegetable oil
1 cup milk
1 tsp nutmeg
Salt and pepper to taste

Directions:

1. Preheat oven to 350°F.
2. Mix all dry ingredients together.
3. Mix egg, milk, and oil into dry mixture and blend well.
4. Pour into 8-inch square pan and bake 30–35 minutes.

Amerindian—a term for the indigenous peoples of North, Central, and South America, including the Caribbean islands, before the arrival of Europeans in the late 15th century.

cay—a low island or reef made from sand or coral.

civil liberty—the right of people to do or say things that are not illegal without being stopped or interrupted by the government.

conquistador—any one of the Spanish leaders of the conquest of the Americas in the 1500s.

Communism—a political system in which all resources, industries, and property are considered to be held in common by all the people, with government as the central authority responsible for controlling all economic and social activity.

coup d'état—the violent overthrow of an existing government by a small group.

deforestation—the action or process of clearing forests.

economic system—the production, distribution, and consumption of goods and services within a country.

ecotourism—a form of tourism in which resorts attempt to minimize the impact of visitors on the local environment, contribute to conserving habitats, and employ local people.

embargo—a government restriction or restraint on commerce, especially an order that prohibits trade with a particular nation.

exploit—to take advantage of something; to use something unfairly.

foreign aid—financial assistance given by one country to another.

free trade—trade based on the unrestricted exchange of goods, with tariffs (taxes) only used to create revenue, not keep out foreign goods.

hurricane—a very powerful and destructive storm, characterized by high winds and significant rainfall, that often occurs in the western Atlantic Ocean and the Caribbean Sea between June and November.

leeward—a side that is sheltered or away from the wind.

mestizo—a person of mixed Amerindian and European (typically Spanish) descent.

offshore banking—a term applied to banking transactions conducted between participants located outside of a country. Such transactions Some Caribbean countries have become known for this practice thanks to their banking laws.

plaza—the central open square at the center of colonial-era cities in Latin America.

plebiscite—a vote by which the people of an entire country express their opinion on a particular government or national policy.

population density—a measurement of the number of people living in a specific area, such a square mile or square kilometer.

pre-Columbian—referring to a time before the 1490s, when Christopher Columbus landed in the Americas.

regime—a period of rule by a particular government, especially one that is considered to be oppressive.

service industry—any business, organization, or profession that does work for a customer, but is not involved in manufacturing.

windward—the side or direction from which the wind is blowing.

Pirate Bios

Write a report on the life of one of the following pirates: Henry Jennings, Edward Teach, Mary Read, or Anne Bonney. Tell how he or she influenced the history of the Bahamas.

"Top Ten" Time Line

Using the chronology in this book, create an illustrated time line to hang in your classroom that displays what you believe are the 10 most important dates in the history of the Bahamas. Be ready to defend your choice of dates to your classmates and teacher.

Travel Brochure

Create a travel brochure for the Bahamas. Include one national park, two major cities, and at least three islands in your brochure. Provide maps and activity guides for your readers.

Maps

- Choose one of the islands of the Bahamas and create a detailed map that shows its bays, towns, cities, elevation variances, and vegetation.

- Create a map that includes as many of the Bahamas islands as possible.

- Research the Mercator projection, a type of map that depicts the globe as a flat surface. Write a paragraph that explains the benefits and drawbacks of this type of map. (Hint: Note the size of Greenland in comparison of South America.).

Spin a Story

Memorize a Bahamian folktale and tell it to your class. Use lively language and feel free to act out the tale as you tell it! Make sure your audience understands the message or moral of your story.

Bahamian Basketball Bio

Research the life of Bahamian Mychal Thompson, a professional basketball player from Harbour Island. Write a report and share it with your classroom teacher and classmates, as well as with your gym teacher.

Groove with Goombay

Research the Bahamian music known as *Goombay*. Try to find a recording of this type of music, or with the help of your music teacher, compose your own *Goombay* tune and perform it for your class!

Ca. 300 CE	First Amerindian settlement in the Bahamas may have occurred.
9th-10th century	The Lucayan tribe of Arawaks settle in the Bahamas.
1492	Columbus lands on San Salvador.
1648	English Puritans from Bermuda form colony on Eleuthera Island.
1650	The golden age of piracy begins.
1670	Britain claims the Bahamas.
1718	Woodes Rogers takes office as the first British royal governor of the Bahamas and begins campaign to drive out the pirates.
1782	Spain briefly recaptures the Bahamas.
1783	The Treaty of Versailles gives back British control of the Bahamas.
1861	Bahamians prosper as they aid Confederate troops during the American Civil War.
1920s	The Bahamas becomes an important—although illegal— supplier of rum during the U.S. Prohibition years.
World War II	The Bahamas islands are used as an important air and sea way station.
1964	Britain grants self-government to the Bahamas.
1969	Britain changes status of Bahamas from colony to commonwealth.
1973	The Bahamas become independent within the Commonwealth of Nations, but retain Queen Elizabeth II as their constitutional head of state.

1980s	United States assists the nation of the Bahamas in a crackdown on illegal drugs.
1992	A pro-business administration led by Hubert A. Ingraham is voted into power.
1997	Ingraham is reelected prime minister.
1999	Hurricanes Dennis and Floyd wreak havoc throughout the islands of the Bahamas.
2002	In May, the Progressive Liberal Party wins the election and Perry Christie becomes the new prime minister of the Bahamas.
2007	The Free National Movement party wins a majority in elections for the House of Assembly, and FNM's Hubert A. Ingraham replaces Perry Christie as prime minister.
2010	In April, Sir Arthur Foulkes is appointed governor-general of the Bahamas.
2012	In parliamentary elections, the Progressive Liberal Party regains power and Perry Christie becomes prime minister again; in October, Hurricane Sandy kills two people and causes $700 million in damage.
2014	The unemployment rate in the Bahamas reaches 15.4 percent; more than 5.5 million people visit the Bahamas.

Matchar, Emily, and Tom Masters. *The Bahamas*. Oakland, Calif.: Lonely Planet, 2014.

Moker, Molly, ed. *In Focus: The Bahamas*. New York: Fodor's Travel Publications, 2008.

Smith, Larry. *The Bahamas: Portrait of an Archipelago*. New York: MacMillan, 2004.

Moya Pons, Frank. *History of the Caribbean: Plantations, Trade, and War in the Atlantic World*. Princeton, N.J.: Markus Wiener Publishers, 2012.

Heuman, Gad. *The Caribbean: A Brief History*. New York: Bloomsbury, 2014.

Barlas, Robert, and Yong Jui Lin. *Bahamas*. New York: Cavendish Square, 2010.

Travel and Tourism

http://www.bahamas.com
http://www.geographia.com/bahamas

History/Geography

http://www.iexplore.com/dmap/Bahamas/history
http://www.interknowledge.com/bahamas/bahistory.htm

Economic/Political

http://www.bahamas.gov.bs
https://www.cia.gov/library/publications/the-world-factbook/geos/bf.html

Culture and Festivals

http://www.myoutislands.com/bahamas-resorts/culture
http://thebahamas.com/jun/index.htm

**Bahamas Ministry of Education,
Science, and Technology**
Thompson Boulevard
P. O. Box N-3913
Nassau, The Bahamas
Tel: 242-502-2700
Fax: 242-322-8491
Web site: http://www.bahamaseducation.com
E-mail info@bahamaseducation.com

The Bahamas Ministry of Tourism
P.O. Box N-3701
Nassau, Bahamas
Tel: 242-302-2000
Toll Free: 1-800-Bahamas
Fax: 242-302-2098
Web site: http://www.bahamas.com
E-mail: tourism@bahamas.com

Embassy of the Bahamas
Ambassador / Permanent Representative
The Bahamas Embassy
2220 Massachusetts Avenue N.W
Washington D.C. 20008
Tel: 202-319-2260
Fax: 202-319-2668
E-mail: jsears@mfabahamas.org

Office of the Prime Minister
Cecil Wallace-Whitfield Centre
Cable Beach
P. O. Box CB-10980
Nassau, N.P., The Bahamas
Tel: 242-327-1530
Fax: 242-327-5806
Web site: http://www.bahamas.gov.bs
E-mail: bis@bahamas.gov.bs

Page
1:    used under license from Shutterstock, Inc.
2:    © OTTN Publishing
3:    © OTTN Publishing
7:    Photo Disc
8:    Dave G. Houser / Houserstock
9:    Dave G. Houser / Houserstock
11:   Dave G. Houser / Houserstock
12:   used under license from Shutterstock, Inc.
14:   Library of Congress
15:   UN Photo
21:   Hulton / Archive / Getty Images
23:   Library of Congress
26:   Getty Images
27:   UN Photo
28:   used under license from Shutterstock, Inc.
29:   Alarico / Shutterstock.com

31:   Dave G. Houser / Houserstock
33:   used under license from Shutterstock, Inc.
34:   Dave G. Houser / Houserstock
35:   Dave G. Houser / Corbis
37:   Tony Arruza / Corbis
40:   Hulton / Archive / Getty Images
41:   Franz-Marc Frei / Corbis
42:   Jonathan Blair / Corbis
43:   Dave G. Houser / Houserstock
45:   Jonathan Blair / Corbis
46:   Tony Arruza / Corbis
51:   Corbis Images

CONTRIBUTORS

Senior Consulting Editor **James D. Henderson** is professor of international studies at Coastal Carolina University. He is the author of *Conservative Thought in Twentieth Century Latin America: The Ideals of Laureano Gómez* (1988; Spanish edition *Las ideas de Laureano Gómez* published in 1985); *When Colombia Bled: A History of the Violence in Tolima* (1985; Spanish edition *Cuando Colombia se desangró, una historia de la Violencia en metrópoli y provincia*, 1984); and coauthor of *A Reference Guide to Latin American History* (2000) and *Ten Notable Women of Latin America* (1978).

Mr. Henderson earned a bachelor's degree in history from Centenary College of Louisiana, and a master's degree in history from the University of Arizona. He then spent three years in the Peace Corps, serving in Colombia, before earning his doctorate in Latin American history in 1972 at Texas Christian University.

Colleen Madonna Flood Williams is the author of more than 10 nonfiction children's books. Colleen resides in Homer, Alaska, with her husband, Paul, son Dillon Meehan, and their dog, Kosmos Kramer.